FRIDA
KAHLO

Maurine Roy

ilex

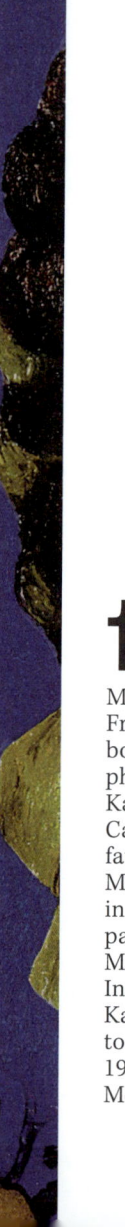

1907

Magdalena Carmen
Frida Kahlo y Calderón is
born, the third daughter of
photographer Guillermo
Kahlo and his wife Matilde
Calderón y Gonzalez. Her
father, who emigrated to
Mexico in 1891, was born
in Germany to Hungarian
parents; her mother was
Mexican, of Spanish and
Indigenous heritage. Frida
Kahlo would later claim
to have been born in
1910, the year of the
Mexican Revolution.

A contentious birth

Magdalena Carmen Frida Kahlo y Calderón, who went by her third given name Frida, derived from the German word for 'peace', was born in Coyoacán, Mexico, on 6 July 1907 to a European immigrant father of German origin and a mother of Spanish and Indigenous heritage. They lived in a lower middle-class neighbourhood in the south of Mexico City and Frida grew up in an almost exclusively female household, comprising three sisters, Cristina, Matilde and Adriana (a brother having died at birth), and two half-sisters from her father's first marriage. Frida got on very differently with her parents, Carl Wilhelm Kahlo (who had styled himself Guillermo upon arrival in Mexico) and Matilde Calderón y Gonzalez; the former encouraged her to think for herself and pushed her to follow her dreams, whereas the latter, an extremely pious and not highly educated woman of conservative leanings, invested very little of herself in young Frida's day-to-day life, although their relationship developed later, as is shown by their warm and tender correspondence.

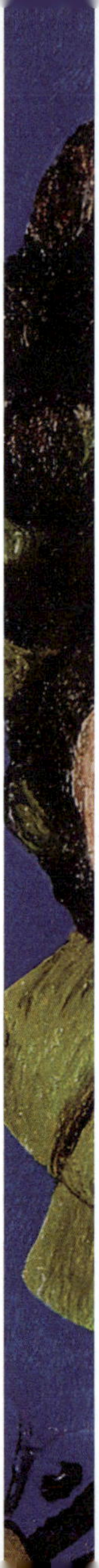

Frida took her father as a role model and source of inspiration, and shared with him a certain vulnerability and the vicissitudes of illness, as he suffered from epileptic seizures. Guillermo Kahlo was the official cultural heritage photographer for the regime of Porfirio Díaz, the dictator deposed in 1911, and shared with Frida his passion for Mexico's art and archaeology, teaching his favourite daughter how to develop, retouch and colourize photographs. Frida's relationship with her mother, who had never really got over the death of her son, was more troubled, however, although she was to forge deep bonds with yet another female figure, namely her nurse.

The complexity of the family circumstances in which Frida grew up was matched only by the political situation that held sway in the country. Mexico was in great turmoil at the time, as a revolution had begun in 1910 that was to transform the country over the course of a decade, bringing Porfirio Díaz's dictatorship to an end. For a long time, Frida would lie about her date of birth, going so far as to claim in her diaries that she had been born on 7 July 1910, as if to cement herself as an icon of this uprising, an emblem of modern Mexico and its cultural melting pot.

She did not come out of her shell until about the age of 15, however, when she transferred to the prestigious Escuela Nacional Preparatoria in the centre of Mexico City. The institution had only just become co-educational and Frida was one of only 35 young women among the two thousand pupils enrolled at the school, already making her a pioneering feminist who was ahead of her time and a national icon as a woman who went on to study medicine

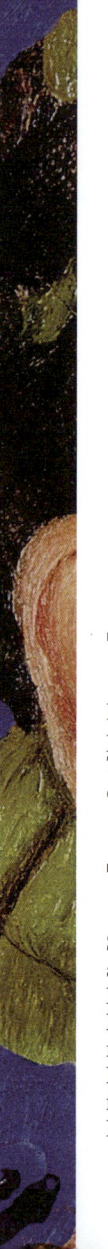

1913

Frida is confined to bed by polio for several months. The illness permanently deforms her right foot.

1923

She attends high school at the prestigious Escuela Nacional Preparatoria in Mexico City where she first meets the artist Diego Rivera, who is painting his fresco *La Creación* in the Bolívar Auditorium.

in a predominantly male world. She may have begun her studies wearing a demure school uniform, but there was no mistaking the young girl's emancipation; Frida forged strong friendships and her small group of classmates, made up of seven boys and two girls, dubbed themselves 'Los Cachuchas' for the caps they wore in protest against their school's strict dress code. With this group she began to fight for political reform within the school, advocating the socio-nationalist ideas of the Mexican revolutionary José Vasconcelos, the incumbent Minister of Education, a key figure who espoused education and literacy for every social class.

A fateful accident

At the age of six, Frida tripped over a root, injuring herself; doctors would later diagnose her with polio, which would affect her gait throughout her life. This loss of mobility attracted ridicule from other children and earned her the nickname 'Frida the lame'. The condition would isolate her from the outside world for most of her childhood, but worse was yet to come. Returning home from school as usual on 17 September 1925, 18-year-old Frida was sitting with Alejandro Gómez Arias, her boyfriend of the time, in the back of one of the crowded buses that traversed the streets of Mexico City. The day was to end in stark tragedy when a tram crashed into the moving bus, crushing it against a wall. The victims were pulled from the wreckage, but Frida's spine was broken, her shoulder dislocated, one leg shattered into pieces and her foot crushed. To compound this horror, an

'The only good
news is that I have
started to get used
to suffering […]'

Letter to Alejandro Gómez Arias,
5 December 1925

1925

On 17 September she is
seriously injured in a traffic
accident that leaves her
disabled and in constant
pain for the rest of her life.
The accident results in
multiple operations,
protracted stays in hospital,
months spent encased in
steel and plaster braces,
several miscarriages and the
later amputation of her
right leg.

1926

She begins to paint and
draw during her
convalescence.

iron rail had impaled her from abdomen to groin. 'It is untrue to say that you notice the shock, untrue to say you cry; I had no tears. The impact pushed us forward and the handrail ran me through the way a sword pierces a bull.' Beauty can sometimes make itself felt at unexpected moments, however, a sachet of gold dust carried by a passenger had burst under the impact and its contents scattered a golden film over the bloodied body of the beautiful Frida. Passers-by, believing a dancer lay on the ground, cried '*la bailarina!*'

This fateful accident in Frida's life turned her relationship with her now ailing and disabled body upside down, and becoming a doctor, as she had once dreamt, was now out of the question; from that point on, she would engage with the medical world only as a patient. 'They are going to change the brace for the third time [...] I will never be able to do anything with this damned affliction, and if that's true at nineteen, I dread to think what it will be like later. I am wasting away, day by day [...] I look dreadful with this enormous, useless brace [...] I now live on a planet of pain, as transparent as ice; but it is as if I had learnt everything all at once, in just a few seconds [...] I have aged in an instant,' she wrote in a letter to Alejandro Gómez Arias in 1926. Frida was bedbound for the majority of her early years and, like Colette or Georges Perec, she made it the focus of her artistic creativity, without ever having anticipated it. She painted because it brought relief, not out of ambition or as some reasoned action; indeed, she did not even ask herself the question: 'I began to paint [...] out of sheer boredom during my year confined to bed after an accident in which I fractured my spine and broke my

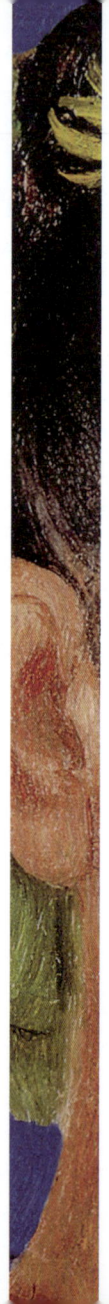

foot and other bones. I had [...] so wanted to study medicine, but everything was denied by a collision between a Coyoacán bus and a Tlalpan tram [...] As I was young, this unfortunate incident did not turn into a tragedy. I had enough energy to do everything other than study medicine and, without realizing it, I began to paint.'

Her parents' life-saving idea of installing an easel in their daughter's room and hanging a mirror above her head necessarily brings up the question of her desire for the Other and her desire for herself. Frida had to learn to love herself again for her own sake, accepting her own fragility and the changes brought about by her condition, but also understanding the image that she presents to others. This was a desire that certainly played a part in her post-traumatic reconstruction of her body image, thanks to the mirror. Self-portraits followed in quick succession; she depicted the traumatic events of her life, just like on votive offerings. Her creations functioned like an autobiography, an intimate diary with her soul laid bare, a kind of dissection of everything in her heart. Painting became an escape route, a door to freedom. 'Long months of agony, and at the end, a rebirth [...] I am nailed down in my bed, unable to stand, crucified by pain and distress. [...] My hands will give me what my legs deny me – escape. I pass through the mirror, moving beyond this prison bed, and I start to paint, paint, paint [...] Frida the artist was born.' While painting was not an early vocation, it was a way of staving off boredom and averting death. Frida was driven by a desperate desire to reconstruct herself, to refashion her image and, above all, to reclaim the ailing body from which she had been alienated

'I'm not sick, I'm broken. But I shall be happy to live as long as I can paint.'

Frida Kahlo's Diary, 1944–1954

1928

Frida meets Italian photographer Tina Modotti, making contact with left-wing intellectuals from literary circles and joining the Communist Party. She bumps into Diego Rivera the same year, and he becomes her life partner.

1929

Diego Rivera and Frida Kahlo marry in August; he is 42, she is 22.

since childhood. Her parents brought her paints and, when canvas did not suffice, Frida painted on her plaster brace, painting to heal herself, painting to survive.

Painting as catharsis

Despite all the relapses, her confinement to bed, the braces and her wheelchair, Frida was determined to pull through, drawing on all her vital energy to reclaim her body and her freedom. She managed to resume a daily life that was practically normal, but from that point on, she devoted herself exclusively to painting. She read voraciously: Proust, Zola, Goethe, Alexander Kerensky's articles on the Russian Revolution, and more. She also took an interest in the painters Lucas Cranach the Elder, Albrecht Dürer and Sandro Botticelli. In 1926, this led her to create *Self-Portrait in a Velvet Dress*, inspired by Italian Renaissance painting, particularly Botticelli, and the Mannerist portraiture typified by Bronzino. She played an active role in the political, cultural and artistic life of her country, meeting with intellectuals and artists, and espoused socialist principles that chimed with the national mood of the time. The person who truly introduced her to communism was Tina Modotti, an Italian photographer and militant revolutionary, thanks to whom Frida became a member of the Young Communist League. Tina also paved Frida's way into Mexico's fashionable art scene, introducing her to the muralist Diego Rivera, whom Frida had in fact already met as a schoolgirl when Rivera had been painting the fresco entitled *La Creación* in

'I wish I could do whatever I liked behind the curtain of "madness". I would then arrange flowers all day long and I would paint; about pain, love and tenderness [...]. I would build my world, which as long as I lived would be in harmony with all the worlds.'

Frida Kahlo's Diary, 1944–54

1930

Frida experiences her first miscarriage. November sees Frida Kahlo and Diego Rivera bound for San Francisco because of Diego's work. They spend four years in the United States, punctuated by brief stays elsewhere. In San Francisco, Frida meets American photographer Edward Weston and Dr Leo Eloesser, whose patient she would become in later years.

the Bolívar Auditorium at her school. Evenings spent at Tina's were unforgettable, with people jostling to see and be seen, dancing, smoking, drinking, arguing and putting the world to rights. From this moment on, Mexican identity and socialism exerted a lasting effect on Frida's thinking, an influence only reinforced by the stormy and tumultuous love affair she would have through the course of her life with Diego, who was also a committed communist.

'I have had two serious accidents in my life; one was when I was hit by a tram, and the other was Diego.' The wedding of the pair, nicknamed 'the elephant and the dove' because of their wildly differing physiques, took place on 21 August 1929. Diego, who was marrying for the third time, nailed his colours to the mast from the outset; he did not believe in fidelity between two people. Frida responded that he would nonetheless be the husband of only one woman, and their intense and passionate relationship is remembered for the numerous extramarital affairs conducted by both parties. Frida also never made a secret of her bisexuality, which caused quite a stir in 1930s bourgeois society.

Frida Kahlo's conflict with her body also spilled over into her life as a woman; it appears she was unable to have children and suffered two successive miscarriages, first in 1930 and then in 1932, during a stay in Detroit, where she had accompanied Diego, who was working on a fresco commission. Her paintings, *Henry Ford Hospital* (1932) and *My Birth* (1932), were directly inspired by these tragic events; in the first, we see the artist lying supine on a large, bloodstained bed, her abdomen still swollen. Frida is surrounded by six different symbolic items, including a male

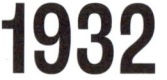

1932

Frida and Diego Rivera
spend several months in
Detroit. Frida's mother
dies on 15 September.

1933

Rivera paints murals in
Detroit and New York.
The couple return to Mexico
City in December, moving
the following year to a
modern duplex in the
suburb of San Angel
(now the Museo Casa
Diego Rivera).

foetus and an orthopaedic model of the pelvic area, attached to her hands by red threads akin to umbilical cords. This painting is one of several that evoke her personal difficulties with fertility as well as her ambivalent feelings towards motherhood, her wish to start a family with Diego Rivera (who fathered several illegitimate children), and the limits of her own body. Frida was certainly not the first person in the history of art to address the theme of pregnancy, but scenes of childbirth and especially miscarriage were still rare and taboo in Western iconography. She was also one of the first women of her time to paint menstrual blood, which was traditionally considered beyond the pale as it was too often associated with impurity and uncleanliness. Additionally, she was the first artist to feature a corpse of a woman stabbed by a jealous husband, a veritable femicide, in the painting *A Few Small Nips*, completed in 1935. The modern interpretation of the picture sees Frida as a fighter for women's rights. Reconstructing her body through painting became a favourite topic and a way of asserting her opinions. By exploring intimacy with her body, Frida made it a political subject, creating a cathartic way of painting and an outlet that spoke to the collective consciousness.

'It must be said of his chest that if he had landed on the island governed by Sappho, he would not have been executed by her warriors. The sensitivity of his marvellous breasts would have rendered him acceptable, although his virility, specific and strange as it was, also made him desirable in the lands of empresses eager for male love.'

'Portrait of Diego', 1949

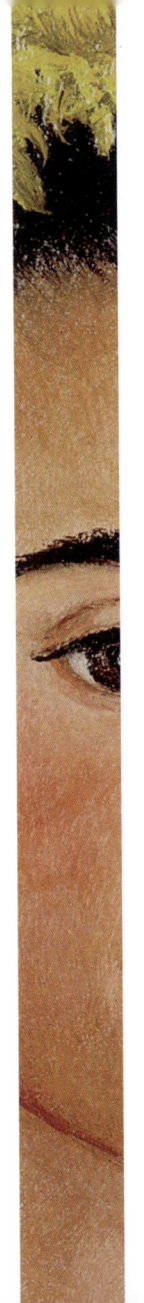

'Extraordinary'

The elephant and the dove, the ogre and the young girl, the toad and the grasshopper: everything seemed to be working against Frida and Diego within this 'monstrous alliance', as the painter's father called it when their wedding was announced. She was young, beautiful and fragile, with a broken body; he was a kind of natural giant with coarse features, and twice her age. Each had a challenges of their own: Frida's was rooted in her disability, whereas Diego's arose from both his physical appearance and his penchant for hurting the women in his life.

The sexual identity between the two lovers may also have been confused; Frida's 'masculine' traits, a luxuriant monobrow and fine black hair on her upper lip, matched Diego's 'feminine' side, the gentleness of his gaze and his fleshy, curvaceous body (whose 'marvellous breasts' Frida lauds in her writings). While Diego Rivera's enormous and unusual physique brought him admiration and interest from the fairer sex, Frida was no wallflower herself. She was a unique woman *sui generis*, defying the norms of her age, with an ability to charm both men and women (including the exiled Communist Leon Trotsky, Nickolas Muray, a Hungarian-born American photographer, the artist Isamu Noguchi and even the dancer Josephine Baker).

The problems arising from her condition, combined with wearing a succession of 28 orthopaedic braces (made of steel, leather or plaster) and the various operations she underwent, made her battered, bruised and abnormal body, like it or not, into a symbol of resistance. Behind the many physical aftershocks, her beautiful, serious and solemn face shines

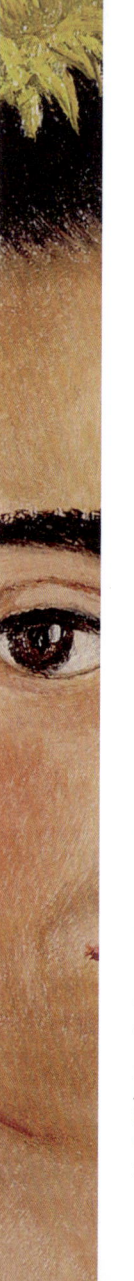

1935

Frida separates from
Diego because of his many
affairs (including one with
her sister, Cristina) and
heads to New York for
several weeks.

1937

The Communist Leon
Trotsky and his wife Natalia
seek refuge in Mexico in
January, initially staying
in Frida's family home, the
Casa Azul (Blue House)
in Coyoacán.

out in her self-portraits as a challenge to the viewer. Even when she paints her body in little pieces, we remain captivated by the unsmiling face, its piercing eyes intensified by eyebrows spread like the wings of a bird. What should we make of these connected eyebrows with which she depicts herself in every one of the 55 self-portraits among her approximately 143 paintings? 'I have the moustache and the general face of the opposite sex,' she said, and, in addition to the impressive stripe above her eyes, she often depicted herself with fine black down on her upper lip. This shadow falling across a mouth that never smiled captures the sexual ambivalence to which she laid claim, a claim that she also maintained with her clothes. Frida loved defying expectations from a very early age.

Clothing and cross-dressing allowed her to create an artistic identity that lay beyond the frontiers of gender. In many photographs, she can be seen posing in male dress for her father's camera. These exposures show the beginnings of the androgyny that the artist was to cultivate throughout her life and her art, although she was also fascinated by the female culture and fashion of the Isthmus of Tehuantepec, a region far from Mexico City where women ran every aspect of society. She retained a taste for richly decorated, ornate headdresses and the magnificently colourful *tehuana* outfits she would wear until the very end of her life, as if she herself had become a living artwork, a goddess. The painting *Self-Portrait with Cropped Hair*, completed in 1940, shows a masculine Frida in a grey suit with a short-back-and-sides, her left hand holding her shorn hair and her right a pair of scissors. The lyrics of a popular Mexican song are written at

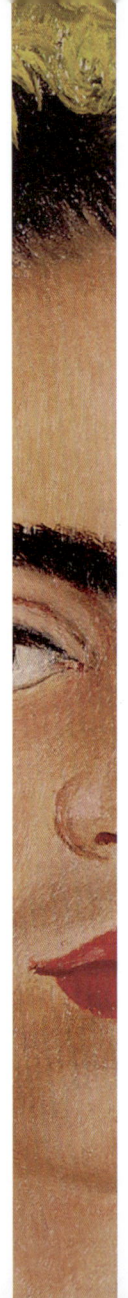

the top of the canvas: '*Mira que si te quise, fué por el pelo, Ahora que estás pelona, ya no te quiero*' (You see, if I loved you, it was because of your hair; now you are bald, I love you no longer). Some historians were immediately tempted to draw a strictly biographical interpretation linking this artwork with the revelation of Diego's extramarital relationship with Cristina, Frida's younger sister. However, the fact of writing it in the work from a perspective of female vengeance reinforces the gender codes that Frida was more than happy to blur.

While the 'extraordinary' nature of this legendary couple is immediately apparent on a physical level, it is also visible in the scope of their work. Drawing an analogy between the respective bodies of Diego and Frida and the dimensions of their creations raises questions, with Diego preferring the grandeur and monumentality of wall painting while frail Frida concentrates on smaller-format canvases. While he paints crowd scenes, she focuses on the individual and more particularly, on herself. This contrast between their artistic approaches has often been seen as the way they operated as a couple, indeed as its essence, with Diego tending to depict the exterior world and Frida the universe of the interior. In Diego's work, we find aspects of abundance and joy in his paintings, *a priori* a world away from Frida's. Each is animated by the same vital force, however, the same impulse that binds them so deeply to one another. By the same token, Diego's interest in his country's pre-Columbian past and indigenous culture also left its mark on Frida's work, and she incorporated elements from Mexican folk art and pre-Hispanic mythology into her canvases, endowing them

'Frida Kahlo de Rivera's art is a ribbon around a bomb.'

André Breton, *Surrealism and Painting*, 1965

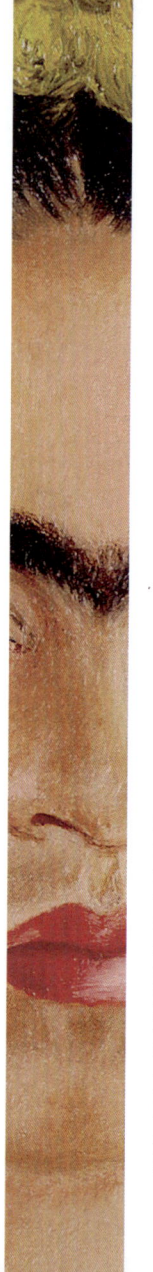

1938

André Breton meets Frida Kahlo during a visit to Mexico and strives to draw her into the Surrealist group. Frida's first solo show, held at Julien Levy's gallery in New York from 25 October to 14 November, is a great success and she sells her first canvases.

First meeting with Hungarian-born American photographer Nickolas Muray.

with an intrinsically national dimension. She also joined the post-revolutionary Mexicayotl movement with its goal of redefining a truly Mexican identity. 'Revolution is the harmony of form and colour. Everything exists and evolves according to a single law, that of life. No one is separate from another, no one fights alone, everything is whole and one. Anguish and pain, pleasure and death, are only a process in existing. The revolutionary struggle in this process is an open door to intelligence,' she wrote in her diary. While it is clearly important to factor in the influence of these elements in our understanding of Frida Kahlo's work, they reveal only the tip of the iceberg of the complexity of her art and of her mind. Frida did not initially have any artistic technique to speak of; while not an absolute beginner, having taken a few sketching classes before her accident, it was her autodidactic spirit that permitted her to quickly master the art of painting and find her own inimitable style.

While Diego earnestly wished to cover every surface in the world with paint, to be invited to the tables of the great and the good, and to enjoy as many sexual conquests as he possibly could, he nonetheless always pushed Frida to outdo him artistically (their successes were very often compared), and he always encouraged her not only to paint but also to make it her profession. He strongly encouraged exhibitions of her work, thereby contributing to her fame, and she would ultimately eclipse him. Rather than Frida being known as 'Diego Rivera's wife', he is now known worldwide as 'Frida Kahlo's husband'.

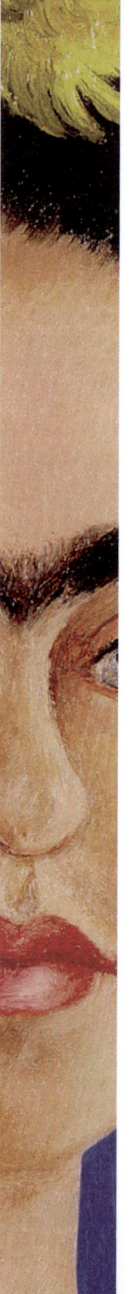

1939

Frida's first trip to Europe.
She receives a rapturous
reception from the
Surrealists in Paris and
Marcel Duchamp organizes
an exhibition of her
paintings among other
Mexican artworks at the
Galerie Renou et Colle.
Diego and Frida divorce on
6 November.

From the real to the imagined body

The transition from the real to the imaginary body undertaken by Frida Kahlo in her painting aligns her with Surrealism. This popular interpretation of her work began with the trip to Mexico by André Breton and his wife Jacqueline Lamba in 1938, the year before Kahlo and Rivera divorced. While the artist's freedom of speech and morality undoubtedly enthused the self-proclaimed 'pope of Surrealism', Breton was principally captivated by Kahlo's painting, although she was much less taken by the theorist's speechifying.

André Breton noted the similarities between the work of the Surrealists and the pictures painted by the Mexican artist, in particular in her canvas *What the Water Gave Me* (1938): the Surrealists saw in this picture details painted with no logical connection between them; an expression, so they liked to maintain, of Frida's unconscious. It was anything but; Kahlo was depicting whole aspects of her biography, as can also be found in older paintings. Her parents can be seen, along with two naked women, one of whom resembles the much-loved nurse of her childhood, the naked body of a dying woman that recalls her miscarriage in 1932, a skeleton symbolizing death as a constant presence in her life, a New York skyscraper in flames, referring to her wish to see the capitalist world disappear, and much more. Although set in a bathtub, this biographical painting is anchored in Frida's reality, rather than freewheeling fantasy; everything is calculated, orchestrated and willed. She would thus decline the label of 'Surrealist' but still accepted an invitation for a solo exhibition in Paris after the resounding

'Surrealism is the magical surprise of finding a lion in a cupboard where you were expecting to find shirts.'

Handwritten note on the reverse of *Fantasía I*, 1944

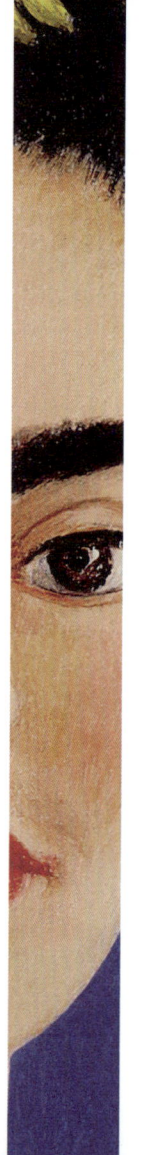

1940

She is featured in the International Exhibition of Surrealism in Mexico City and the major 'Twenty Centuries of Mexican Art' exhibition in New York. Leon Trotsky is assassinated in Coyoacán, Mexico City, on 21 August. Frida Kahlo travels to San Francisco to consult Dr Eloesser, partly because of her growing problem with alcoholism. Frida Kahlo and Diego Rivera marry in San Francisco for a second time on 8 December.

success of her first retrospective exhibition at Julien Levy's gallery in New York in October 1938.

Her trip to Paris was a disaster, according to her diaries and her correspondence with her lover, Nickolas Muray, who had stayed in New York. Breton failed to keep his promises; there was no Parisian gallery waiting for her, and French intellectuals failed to make a good impression on her: 'They have so many crappy intellectuals that I can no longer stand. They're really just too much for me. [...] I'd rather be sat on the floor selling tortillas in Toluca market than have anything to do with those artistic idiots from Paris [...]' Frida's solo exhibition was ultimately turned into a group show at the Galerie Renou et Colle but her works were swamped by a pile of things that Breton had brought back from Mexico; folk art and naïve-style paintings were thrown in among objects of all kinds, such as pre-Columbian sculptures and photographs, and Kahlo's works struggled to find a place. Despite this, she attracted many admirers, not least Pablo Picasso (who was so impressed he gifted her some earrings) and Elsa Schiaparelli, who entitled one of her creations *Madame Rivera*. Frida's star was shining ever brighter. As Wassily Kandinsky related to his friends Anna and Josef Albers on 17 March 1939, 'We are having an exhibition of Mexican art at the moment. There are fragments of ancient Mexican art and sculptures that are very interesting [...] as well as lots of folk art, and finally, a large number of paintings by Diego Rivera's wife, with a strong Surrealist feel. She was present in person, in Mexican dress, very picturesque. It seems she goes about like that everywhere. There were lots of ladies who looked rather

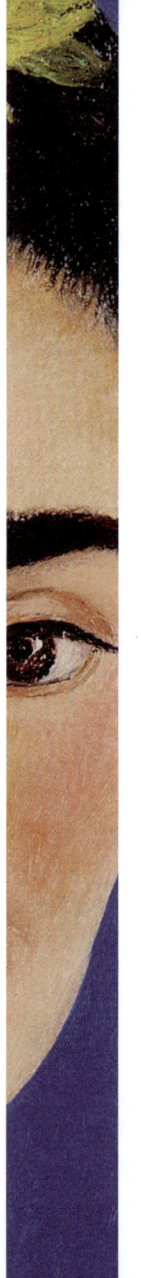

1941

Frida's father dies on
14 April and she returns
to Mexico.

1943

She gives classes at the
Esmeralda school of
painting and sculpture
and the courses soon switch
location to the Casa Azul.
A group of her students
known as *Los Fridos*
rapidly make a name
for themselves.

eccentric – the spirit of Montparnasse – but none to rival the Mexican costume [...].'

'I am not a Surrealist and have never painted dreams. I have painted my own reality. All I know is that I paint because I need to and I always paint whatever comes into my head, with no other consideration.' Frida did not concentrate on her dreams or nightmares and did not seek inspiration in delirium or hallucination, as Max Ernst and Salvador Dalí were able to. Instead, she drew on her day-to-day life and her own reality: her complex path ever since birth, her complicated marriage to Diego and his many infidelities, her membership of the Mexican community, her future political aspirations and more. The body she painted was not so different from her actual body, as it addressed her own feelings, and while these feelings remained personal, they were universally understood.

Representing pain

Whether she chose to or not, Frida Kahlo became an icon of female suffering and resilience. Although she may have exorcized her pain in her paintings and it is easy to see the therapeutic and cathartic virtues of her work, care must be taken not to trap her within an ableist stereotype of the 'poor disabled person'. The medical world was part and parcel of her daily life from childhood on, and was a natural source of inspiration, as were communist values or Mexican identity, for example. In addition, a comparison of Frida's biography with the dates her works were completed confirms that most

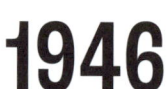

1946

Mexico's Ministry of Education awards her second prize at an art exhibition and a government grant to her picture *Moses*.

1950

She spends a year in hospital in Mexico City.

of her paintings were produced during the most difficult periods in her life, rendering her life and work inseparable.

Although Frida depicts herself by turns as a Christian martyr, Our Lady of Sorrows, shot through with arrows like St Sebastian, and a victim of Aztec sacrifice, she is painting her own reality. She shows the blood running down her legs and bares her forehead to reveal Diego or death there. In *The Broken Column* (1944), she opens up her body, which is studded with nails, and depicts herself for the first time with the steel brace she was obliged to wear after yet another surgical operation. Tears may be running down her cheeks, but it is a depiction not of sadness but rather of the deep and invisible pain of her battered body. A representation of Frida's mind can also be seen in her rebellious and penetrating gaze, which challenges the viewer as if to exclaim, 'don't be afraid of this body!' Frida Kahlo's works, and her self-portraits in particular, are triumphant affirmations of life, not just some accumulation of physical suffering. As a kind of survival, her art helped her to get back on her feet and, though it is difficult to show perpetual change in a painting, Frida managed to capture her relationship with her body, her inner pain, underlined with a broad streak of humour, bright colours and symbolism (that would bring her closer to the Surrealist group). Her correspondence reveals that she was endlessly amusing in the face of illness and death.

The canvases that translate physical pain have counterparts in many paintings that express moral suffering. In her work, the period between 1935 and 1940 appears to have been the most painful of her life. She painted *Memory,*

'Mexico hasn't changed. It's in a hell of a mess; all that's left is the immense beauty of the land and the Indians. The dirty United States steals a little bit every day, it's really sad, but people need to eat, so that's just the way it is, the big fish eats the smallest.'

Letter to Dr Leo Eloesser, 14 June 1931

1953

Frida Kahlo's first solo exhibition in Mexico City is held at the Galería de Arte Contemporáneo. She is gravely ill but attends the opening lying on her four-poster bed. Her right leg is amputated on 27 April.

1954

She attends a demonstration on 2 April for Guatemala in a wheelchair.

Frida Kahlo dies at the Casa Azul on 13 July at the age of 47.

the Heart (1937) to address the double betrayal she suffered in 1934 when her husband had an affair with her younger sister Cristina, depicting herself with a tearful face and a gaping hole in place of her heart, which lies bleeding, in a final spasm, at her feet. Pain is also present in her diary; Frida wrote, drew and painted, recording certain political and aesthetic ideas, her infinite love for Diego, and commenting on the suffering she had endured. The diary covers the last ten years of her life and is a valuable record of her relationship with illness, from her last surgical operations (which prevented her from continuing the courses she had been giving at the National School of Painting, Sculpture and Printmaking) to the gangrene that was to take her right leg below the knee. Frida insisted on attending the opening of her first solo exhibition in Mexico City in the spring of 1953, whatever the cost. She made her appearance lying down, having been carried on a stretcher from home to lie on her own four-poster bed, which had been specially transported to the gallery. She was to die of pneumonia the following year, at the age of 47.

Frida Kahlo's fame, which only grew after her death in 1954 (even coming to be known as 'Fridamania'), gave rise to differing perceptions of the artist. She was a liberated woman with a life fraught with difficulty, but how did she become both an artistic and a feminist icon? It may have been because her artistic and social engagement shone a spotlight on taboo subjects, denouncing patriarchal and societal norms. She was an advocate of pleasure, equality and liberty for all women, and it is interesting to wonder whether Frida, during her lifetime, was aware that the

'Her canvases conveyed a vital sensuality that was further enhanced by powers of observation that were merciless, yet sensitive. It was clear to me that this young girl was a true artist.'

Diego Rivera, on Frida Kahlo's painting

1957
Diego Rivera dies on 24 November in Mexico City.

1958
The Museo Frida Kahlo opens in the Casa Azul in Coyoacán on 30 July.

positions she adopted tended to be anti-conformist. There was no mistaking her feminism in her private life; this necessarily had repercussions for her creative imagination, and her legacy seems undeniable today. Her refusal to share her personal space with Diego, a man, her emancipation from a physical point of view as a woman, indeed a disabled woman, her left-wing, nationalist convictions, which she spread via seemingly innocuous paintings, all go to show that she was ahead of her time and that our 21st-century understanding finds a resonance in her canvases. With their focus on representation of the self, Frida's works ask questions about reflection, identity and belonging to a gender, all of which are ideas of great relevance in our modern, image-orientated society. It is undoubtedly this perception of a liberal, female artist, rightly wielding the power to decide her own image and liberating herself from the social dogmas of the conservative Mexico of the 1930s to the 1950s, that has made her a true icon of the feminist movements of the late 20th century. Frida loved to be photographed, seen and admired, and she loved to be talked about; she had an exact notion of who she was and of the aesthetic universe she wished to reveal to the gaze of whoever encountered her or observed her work. 'Our passage through this world is so absurd and ephemeral that the only thing that reassures me is the knowledge that I have been authentic . . . have been the person most like myself that I could imagine,' she wrote in her diary. Frida: or the construction of a myth that is nowhere near dying out.

The Frame

It's market day in Santa Catarina in the state of Oaxaca. Frida
Kahlo has set her heart on a little frame made from coloured
glass for sale by a stallholder. The hand-made glass frame,
which was intended to hold a mirror, a photo portrait or a
religious icon like Mexican votive offerings, would be used
to enclose a famous self-portrait, painted in the centre of a
block of blue (that is reminiscent of the Casa Azul of her
childhood) on a thin sheet of aluminium. The artist's face
appears encircled by varieties of flowers and exotic birds
like a Madonna in a mandorla. The bright colour palette
recalls Frida's familiar pre-Columbian accessories and votive
objects, and there is a striking clash in feeling between the
set, severe face that is typical of her self-portraits and the
burgeoning flora and fauna in this festive and joyful roundel.
Frida Kahlo's artistic universe also inhabits this duality,
as if depicting abundant life represented cheating death
and illness.

Self-portraiture occupies an essential place within her
painting: 'I paint myself because I am the person I know best.'
She mainly created depictions of herself, but also produced
autobiographical paintings, canvases representing episodes
in her life, along with the occasional portrayal of herself in
the metaphorical form of a wounded animal. Her renowned
self-portraits are much more than her iconic monobrow
because they can be seen as masks, the masks of a persona
she had been fashioning all her life as she rejected all the
ideas upheld by social norms. In *The Frame* (1938), Frida has
clearly chosen to blend her identity with artisanal creativity
and with her roots, as if she were erasing herself in some

'To feel in my own pain the pain of all those who suffer, and to draw my courage from the necessity of living to fight on their behalf.'

Handwritten poem, *ca.* 1950–7

way behind traditional Mexican decoration and the surrounding frame. The very name of the painting also refers to its original enclosure and says much about Frida's personal history, far removed from Surrealism and the Paris scene of the 1930s that she frequented for a while at the invitation of André Breton, who chose to exhibit this painting along with 17 of the artist's other works displayed at the Galerie Renou et Colle.

The exhibition closed in March 1939, and Frida returned to New York, but the small colourful picture remained in Paris. It was purchased by the French state two months later and added to the collections housed in the Jeu de Paume arts centre with the title 'Portrait of the Artist – a painting by Mrs Frida de Rivera'. No further paintings were to be added to this museum's collections (it was used by the Nazis to store artworks looted from Jewish collectors during the Second World War) and the small self-portrait did not reappear until the end of the 1970s, when the collections from France's national Museum of Modern Art in the Palais de Tokyo were transferred to the Pompidou Centre, which remains the only European museum to hold a work by the artist in its permanent collection.

WHERE TO SEE KAHLO'S WORK

In France
· Pompidou Centre, Paris:
  The Frame

In Mexico
· Eighteen of her works are preserved
  in the Frida Kahlo Museum in the
  Casa Azul in Coyoacán, Mexico
  City, along with all her archives
  (in particular, her wide-ranging
  correspondence, her meticulously
  annotated books, her collections of
  Mexican folk and pre-Columbian art,
  and her father's photographs)
· Museo Dolores Olmedo, Mexico City
· Museo de Arte Moderno, Mexico City

PUBLICATIONS
· *The Diary of Frida Kahlo: An Intimate
  Self-Portrait*, Abrams, 2006
· Hayden Herrera, *Frida: The Biography
  of Frida Kahlo*, Bloomsbury, 2018
· Christina Burrus, *Frida Kahlo:
  'I Paint my Reality' (New Horizons),*
  Thames and Hudson, 2008

WATCH
· *Frida*, biopic by Julie Taymor with
  Salma Hayek in the lead role, Studio
  Canal, 2002
· *Frida Kahlo, Between Passion and
  Pain*, documentary by Rodrigo
  Castano Valencia and Ana Vivas,
  Films du Village, 2001

PODCASTS
· *Frida Kahlo, In Our Time*,
  BBC Radio 4, 9 July 2015
· *Short History of Frida Kahlo,*
  20 March 2023

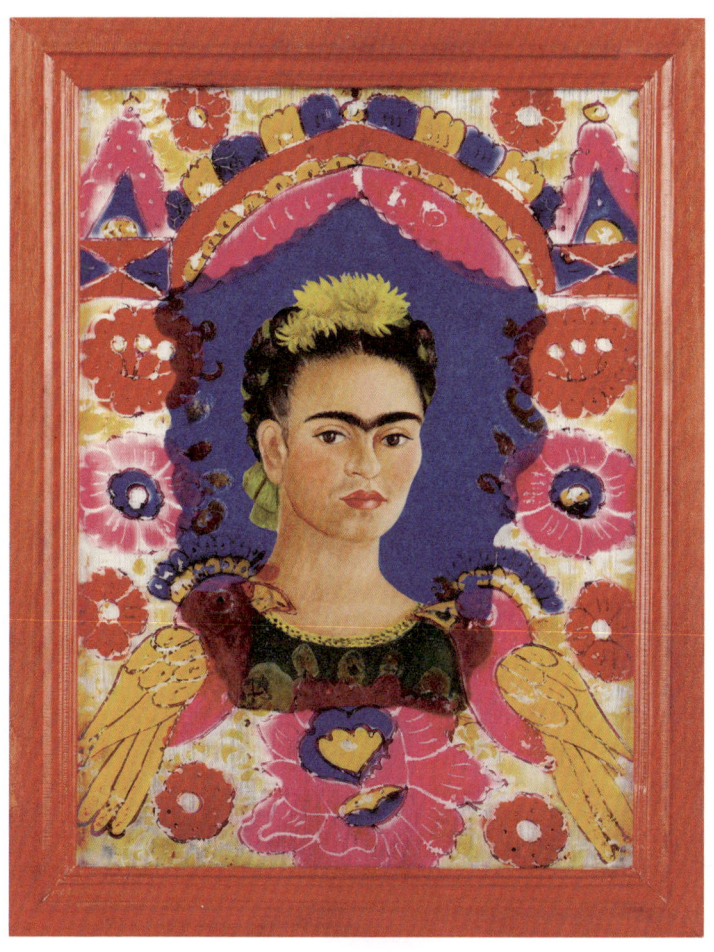

Frida Kahlo, *The Frame*, 1938, oil on aluminium, 28.5 × 20.7cm (11¼ × 8¼ inches),
Pompidou Centre, National Museum of Modern Art – Centre de création industrielle, Paris

Maurine Roy is an art historian specializing in the representation of the body in modern and contemporary art. She is currently an Assistant Curator and has created the podcast *Dessine-moi un corps*.